To:

_____

From:

_____

"Blessed is the God and Father of our Lord Jesus Christ, who has blessed us with every spiritual blessing in the heavenly realms in Christ. For he chose us in Christ before the foundation of the world that we may be holy and unblemished in his sight in love."

Ephesians 1:3-4

For my amazing wife Meredith
who inspires me to be more like Jesus in my daily walk

DAILY GROWTH JOURNAL

Grow in Christ by journaling 10 minutes a day

Chris Lamberth

Second edition

Contents

Introduction

WELCOME TO THE DAILY GROWTH JOURNAL!

I'm excited you've chosen to embark on this journey of growth in your walk with Christ. The journal is straightforward and doesn't require much instruction. So you can jump right in and get started if you wish. However, in this intro I want to share with you how this journal came to be, how it can help you grow in your walk with Christ, and how to get the most out of it.

WHY I CREATED THE DAILY GROWTH JOURNAL

I've always wanted to keep a journal. I knew the practice of regularly journaling was an important discipline because some of history's greatest leaders, both inside and outside of the church, have kept journals throughout their lives. It's a discipline that can be linked with increased productivity, better emotional health, and a greater sense of life purpose. It also provides an outlet to explore your innermost feelings and discover what is truly important to you. But even though I knew how much a journal could enrich my life, I couldn't seem to find the time to stay consistent.

Before the Daily Growth Journal I only managed to journal consistently when I was required to for a class assignment. But even then I still found it difficult to journal on a regular basis. I would have to go back to fill in the days I'd missed just to complete the assignment. This took the joy out of journaling. It felt more like a chore than an opportunity for growth.

But during those rare moments when I actually made time to journal, I enjoyed it. Journaling gave me an outlet to share my thoughts, vent about the day, think through tough issues, and reflect on my life without judgement from others. My favorite part, though, was looking back over entries months or years later. Doing so gave me a profound sense of satisfaction as I saw how I'd grown and overcome obstacles in my life. It allowed me to see in a more objective way, giving me clarity to review my life, learn from my mistakes, and praise God for the victories.

But even all these benefits couldn't help me become a consistent journaler. I would try buying new journals hoping they would motivate me. I created schedules and set alarms reminding me to write, but nothing seemed to work. Then, I came across some journals designed so that writing in them only took a few minutes each day. They made this possible by asking simple, yet powerful questions on each day's page. When I saw this, I immediately said, "I want a Christian version of that!" So I set out to create a journal for myself that would stimulate real spiritual growth, but only take a few minutes every day. That meant the journal prompts had to be laser focused on the most important areas of the Christian life in order for the journal to produce growth in mine.

As I researched ways to create the best—but shortest—journal, I realized I had to share this with the world. For the first time in my life, I was journaling several times a week! And not only that, I noticed a remarkable difference in how my day went when I journaled compared to when I didn't. As I experimented and answered those prompts—many of which are now found in this journal—I felt a greater sense of purpose, which caused me to be more focused on my daily work and inspired me to serve others. I became more mindful of God's presence in my life and aware of the opportunities around me to act as His hands and feet.

I found the gratitude prompt especially helpful. I've struggled with depression for most of my life, so intentionally taking time to reflect on the things I have to be grateful for filled my days with more joy and happiness than I ever thought possible. This exercise has taught me that no matter what I may be going through, there is always something for which I can be grateful. Gaining this perspective has allowed me to persevere through some of life's most difficult moments, even the death of my mother.

My experience with using this journal has taught me that God is always with me, that He gives good gifts even in the midst of incredible pain, and that He has a plan and purpose for my life. I believe this to be true about your life as well, and I am sure you will experience the same assurances through God's work in your life as you use this journal to deepen your walk with Him.

I know that if this journal helped me so much in just a few short months, others who have experienced the same problems keeping a journal, or who simply want to go deeper in their relationship with Christ, will benefit as well.

Some people enjoy spending 30 minutes or more journaling, and I applaud them! This journal is not for them (although they would still benefit from it). I created the Daily Growth Journal (DGJ) for people who want to enjoy the benefits of journaling but have difficulty with keeping a traditional journal. This journal is also perfect if you want to begin journaling for the first time but don't know where to start.

How it Works

The DGJ exists to guide you through simple reflections each day that focus on the most essential aspects of the Christian life: gratitude, identity in Christ, service to others, prayer, mindfulness, and surrender. Intentionally reflecting on these areas in your life is what is known as "mindfulness."

As you develop mindfulness in your life you'll become more aware of your thoughts and feelings. You'll become more aware of what God is doing in the world around you and more sensitive to His Spirit as He calls you to be like

Him and empowers you to serve others. By practicing mindfulness, we focus on the present moment so our thoughts and behavior are less reactive. Rather than responding to every negative stimuli or thinking about the next task, the next job, or the next meal, we learn to focus on the present and to be thankful for what God has blessed us with. This gives us clarity and insight to see the needs of those around us so we can act to bring about meaningful change.

The DGJ will help you become intentionally aware of God's presence, voice, and blessings in your life. This journal can't force you to grow. You must earnestly reflect and choose to focus on what God is doing in your life. As this happens, you will want to follow Him more. Your behavior will begin to look more like His. You will naturally want to sin less and live a righteous life. The Holy Spirit will transform your heart so that your desires will become like His.

THE BEST WAY TO USE THE DAILY GROWTH JOURNAL

The journal was designed to have two main areas for reflection: the daily and the weekly reflections. The daily pages ask you to focus on what God is doing in your life in the current moment. The weekly reflections ask broader questions so you can spot patterns and see how God is working in your life. This will help you gain perspective on the trajectory of your life and remind you of the greater scope of your spiritual life. The daily pages look like this:

Date: _____

"Calling is not only a matter of being and doing what we are but also of becoming what we are not yet but are called by God to be."
—Os Guinness

I am thankful for . . .
1. _____
2. _____
3. _____

God is calling me to be . . .

I can serve God and others today by . . .

My prayer for today is . . .

Where or how did I see God at work today?

What did I struggle with today that I want to overcome tomorrow?

Your Notes

"I, therefore, the prisoner for the Lord, urge you to live worthily of the calling with which you have been called."
Ephesians 4:1

The questions and layout have been left general so you can respond to the questions based on your unique circumstances. For most, journaling when life is good seems to be the most difficult. But the short, easy to answer questions help keep you motivated to journal even when you don't feel like going deep.

DAILY GROWTH REFLECTION

Prime Your Reflection

Each day's reflection begins with a quote. These aren't your typical inspirational quotes. They will challenge you to think deeply about what it means to be a Christian. Take a few moments before you begin journaling to reflect on what the quote says. You can meditate on this throughout the day.

Next is a series of short questions. (Example below). You'll notice the journal asks the same questions each day. But this is purposeful. While the questions don't change, your answers will. Each question has been designed specifically to touch on an essential aspect of the Christian life, but left general enough to allow for flexibility in your answers each day. You will be challenged to reflect deeply and think about the same questions in different ways. This is what produces growth!

I am thankful for . . .

1. my amazing wife and two beautiful daughters.
2. God's grace and patience with me.
3. resources and opportunities to grow in Christ.

God is calling me to be . . .

a spiritual leader to those around me. This means I need to not be afraid of what others think of me, but be confident in the person God has called me to be.

I can serve God and others today by . . .

Inviting my unsaved friend out to eat with me and some others from the church so he can see we are just ordinary people who love God and care about him.

My prayer for today is . . .

that the Holy Spirit would guide me throughout the day and help me see the opportunities He puts in front of me to be used by Him.

Where or how did I see God at work today?

I had to present at an important meeting. I was afraid my ideas would be rejected. But God helped me get through the meeting, and everyone was receptive to what I had to say.

What did I struggle with today that I want to overcome tomorrow?

I struggled with feelings of fear and anxiety of being rejected. I want to rest in confidence knowing that I'm a child of God.

On the day's second page is room to expand your answer if needed or to customize your experience by writing your own notes. One day you may need to explore the big mysteries of the Christian life or struggle to find what God is calling you to do with your life. Other days you might need to focus on one specific task that God has asked you to do. This journal allows you to explore your thoughts and feelings all the way from, "I feel God is calling me to be a missionary to a foreign land," to "I feel God is calling me to help my neighbor in their yard."

Finally, each day is followed up by a Scripture passage. Reflect on the quote in light of Scripture. By reflecting on these quotes in relation to what Scripture says, you'll condition yourself to make this a natural part of your thinking process. It doesn't matter whether you're reading a Christian self-help book or watching a TED Talk. You should always ask, "What does this mean in light of Scripture?"

You'll also notice that the journal pages allow you to add your own date. That means you don't have to start the journal on a particular day. You don't even have to do it every day! Of course, you'll see more benefits the more you use it. But if you miss a day, NO PROBLEM! Don't worry about going back and trying to fill in days you miss (unless that's the way you like to journal). Just pick up your journaling on whatever day it happens to be. You might find you journal best once or twice a week. If that's the case, go for it! Use this journal as a tool to help you grow. Journaling is a spiritual discipline, but don't let the pursuit of perfection become the enemy of progress.

DAILY QUESTIONS

Six daily questions require you to think deeply on an important aspect of Christian life.

1. Gratitude

Studies have shown that gratitude training is one of the biggest producers of happiness in a person's life. As Christians, we have more reason than anyone to be thankful because we enjoy the benefits of salvation. We have access to the God of the universe who provides unparalleled peace, provision, joy, and so much more. Answering this question will fill you with gratitude and set the tone for a worshipful day.

Answering this question every day means you will have to move past the same few answers you would typically give. Your goal should be to look for the little things you are thankful for, not just the big ones. Thankfulness produces happiness! There is always something to be thankful for, no matter what we may be experiencing.

2. Identity in Christ

Who are you in Christ, and who has He called you to be? No question matters more than this one. Our identity in Christ should shape our entire life. How we see ourselves determines the purpose of our lives. Understanding your identity in Christ is the most important step of growing in Him. How can you become more like Him if you don't understand your identity in Him? If you have accepted Jesus Christ as your Lord and Savior, your identity now rests in Him as a child of God and His true righteousness has been accounted to you. God has declared you are in right relationship with Him because of Jesus' death and resurrection (see Romans 3:20-26 and Romans 5:1-11).

While you should never forget that your ultimate identity is in Christ as a child of God, your answers to this question don't have to solely focus on this point. Explore how your identity in Christ plays itself out in daily life. There may be weeks when you just need to reaffirm that you are a child of God, but I hope you'll be more specific as well. God may be calling you to be obedient to something He has asked of you. He may be calling you to be a servant, or a missionary, or a better wife or husband. Whatever the case may be, this question should allow you to explore who God has created you to be and what impact that knowledge has on your life.

3. Service

Service is about going from *being* to *doing*. As a child of God, you are called to bless others by serving them. Jesus said, "Whoever wants to be great among you must be your servant, and whoever wants to be first among you must be your slave—just as the Son of Man did not come to be served but to serve, and to give his life as a ransom for many" (Matthew 20:26-28). Serving God and others is the natural extension of our being children of God. Service doesn't have to be leading someone to the Lord, (although that is wonderful!). Sometimes the simplest tasks of going to work and letting your light shine before others is the best way for you to model Christ before others.

4. Prayer

All the reflection in the world does not prepare us to be like Christ unless we are spending time in His presence. Prayer is when we get to come directly before God, pour out our hearts, and hear Him speak directly to us. Your answer to this question obviously won't be your entire prayer time. It's meant to be a place to either summarize what you have prayed during your time with God, or a place to write specific needs for the day.

5. *Mindfulness*

Where is God working and what is He doing in your life? Answering this is one of the best exercises for developing mindfulness because it's directly related to being aware of God's presence in your life. Some days you'll find it hard to answer this question, and that's okay. You may even feel guilty for not having a good answer (as I have). Don't! This question will encourage you to pay even more attention to God's workings throughout the day. As you struggle to find answers, you will grow in His presence. You will begin to see Him in the little moments, not just the big ones.

6. *Surrender*

Reflect back over the day and look for behaviors, attitudes, or situations that you struggled with that you'd like to overcome tomorrow. This will teach you to surrender those areas of struggle to God and to walk in His grace. By writing out the issue you're struggling with, it will help you be mindful of what caused your struggle and lead you to insights on how to avoid temptation, better control your behavior, and walk in the power of the Holy Spirit so you can overcome that struggle.

YOUR NOTES

This section was added so you can continue to write and further reflect on any of the above areas as needed. Some days, simple answers will suffice. Other days, you'll find you need more room to explore what God is doing in your life or to document the fresh insights or breakthroughs you've had. This is also a great place to jot down ideas throughout the day or take notes on your daily Bible reading. You may also want to eventually begin adding your own prompts to your daily routine. It will help you develop your journaling ability so you can begin exploring other forms of journaling and customize it however you like.

WEEKLY GROWTH CHECK-INS

Every seven days you'll encounter a weekly growth check-in and a challenge for the upcoming week. These are designed to help break up the routine of the daily questions and to challenge you to grow deeper in specific aspects of the Christian life. You'll encounter challenges that range from prayer and Bible reading all the way to finding a mentor and personal leadership development.

While the weekly check-ins give you a break from the daily questions, you'll find that several of the questions stay the same from week to week. Similar to the daily growth questions, the weekly questions will spur you to reflect and evaluate your life over an entire week.

The challenges are meant to get you out of your comfort zone and stimulate growth in other areas of your life not covered in the daily reflections. For example, you will be challenged to read more Scripture one week while another challenges you to break a bad habit by replacing it with a positive one.

FREE-JOURNAL PAGES

In the back of this journal I've provided several blank pages specifically for when you need more free space outside of the normal daily pages to write, add notes, or even doodle your thoughts.

SPIRITUAL GROWTH IS WAITING. LET'S GET STARTED!

Now that you have an understanding of how the journal works, there's nothing left to do but get started. It is my sincere prayer that the Holy Spirit guides you as you embark on this incredible journey of growth!

Your Daily Growth Starting Point

Are you happy with your life right now? Why or why not?

_____

_____

_____

_____

How do you feel about your spiritual progress right now?

_____

_____

_____

_____

What do you think is your life's purpose?

_____

_____

_____

_____

In what areas of your life do you most want to grow?

_____

_____

_____

_____

What do you hope to get out of this journal?

_____

_____

_____

_____

Date: _____ _____

"Calling is not only a matter of being and doing what we are but also of becoming what we are not yet but are called by God to be."
—Os Guinness

I am thankful for . . .

1. _____
2. _____
3. _____

God is calling me to be . . .

_____
_____
_____

I can serve God and others today by . . .

_____
_____
_____

My prayer for today is . . .

_____
_____
_____

Where or how did I see God at work today?

_____
_____

What did I struggle with today that I want to overcome tomorrow?

_____
_____
_____

Your Notes

_____
_____
_____
_____
_____
_____
_____
_____
_____
_____
_____
_____
_____
_____
_____
_____
_____
_____
_____
_____
_____
_____
_____
_____
_____

"I, therefore, the prisoner for the Lord, urge you to live
worthily of the calling with which you have been called."

Ephesians 4:1

Date: _____

"There is not one blade of grass, there is no color in this world that is not intended to make us rejoice."
—John Calvin

I am thankful for . . .

1. _____
2. _____
3. _____

God is calling me to be . . .

_____
_____
_____

I can serve God and others today by . . .

_____
_____
_____

My prayer for today is . . .

_____
_____
_____

Where or how did I see God at work today?

_____
_____

What did I struggle with today that I want to overcome tomorrow?

_____
_____
_____

Your Notes

_____

_____

_____

_____

_____

_____

_____

_____

_____

_____

_____

_____

_____

_____

_____

_____

_____

_____

_____

_____

_____

_____

_____

"This is the day the Lord has brought about. We will be happy and rejoice in it."

Psalm 118:24

Date: _____

_____

"As we allow Christ's character to be formed in us—as we think and act like Jesus—others come under the loving influence of the kingdom and eventually their own hearts are won over to the King of Kings."
—Gregory Boyd

☀

I am thankful for . . .

1. _____
2. _____
3. _____

God is calling me to be . . .

_____
_____
_____

I can serve God and others today by . . .

_____
_____
_____

My prayer for today is . . .

_____
_____
_____

☾

Where or how did I see God at work today?

_____
_____

What did I struggle with today that I want to overcome tomorrow?

_____
_____
_____

Your Notes

_____

_____

_____

_____

_____

_____

_____

_____

_____

_____

_____

_____

_____

_____

_____

_____

_____

_____

_____

_____

_____

_____

_____

_____

"Only conduct yourselves in a manner worthy of the gospel of Christ so that—
whether I come and see you or whether I remain absent—I should hear that
you are standing firm in one spirit, with one mind, by contending side by side
for the faith of the gospel."

Philippians 1:27

Date: _____ _____

"When man is with God in awe and love, then he is praying."
—Karl Rahner

I am thankful for . . .

1. _____
2. _____
3. _____

God is calling me to be . . .

_____
_____
_____

I can serve God and others today by . . .

_____
_____
_____

My prayer for today is . . .

_____
_____
_____

Where or how did I see God at work today?

_____
_____

What did I struggle with today that I want to overcome tomorrow?

_____
_____
_____

Your Notes

_____

_____

_____

_____

_____

_____

_____

_____

_____

_____

_____

_____

_____

_____

_____

_____

_____

_____

_____

_____

_____

_____

_____

_____

_____

"Always rejoice, constantly pray, in everything give thanks.
For this is God's will for you in Christ Jesus."

Thessalonians 5:16-18

Date: _____   _____

"We fear men so much, because we fear God so little."
—William Gurnall

I am thankful for . . .

1. _____
2. _____
3. _____

God is calling me to be . . .

_____
_____
_____

I can serve God and others today by . . .

_____
_____
_____

My prayer for today is . . .

_____
_____
_____

Where or how did I see God at work today?

_____
_____
_____

What did I struggle with today that I want to overcome tomorrow?

_____
_____
_____

Your Notes

_____

_____

_____

_____

_____

_____

_____

_____

_____

_____

_____

_____

_____

_____

_____

_____

_____

_____

_____

_____

_____

_____

_____

_____

_____

_____

_____

_____

"The beginning of wisdom is to fear the Lord, and acknowledging the
Holy One is understanding."

Proverbs 9:10

Date: _____ _____

"*Spiritual direction is an interpersonal relationship in which we learn
how to grow, live, and love in the spiritual life.*"
—*Richard Foster*

I am thankful for . . .

1. _____
2. _____
3. _____

God is calling me to be . . .

_____
_____
_____

I can serve God and others today by . . .

_____
_____
_____

My prayer for today is . . .

_____
_____
_____

☾

Where or how did I see God at work today?

_____
_____
_____

What did I struggle with today that I want to overcome tomorrow?

_____
_____
_____

Your Notes

_____

_____

_____

_____

_____

_____

_____

_____

_____

_____

_____

_____

_____

_____

_____

_____

_____

_____

_____

_____

_____

_____

_____

_____

"Make me know Your ways, O LORD; Teach me Your paths.
Lead me in Your truth and teach me, For You are the God of my salvation;
For You I wait all the day."

Psalm 25:4-5

Weekly Growth Check-In

"Don't just ask God for what we want. Let him teach us what we should want."
—Kevin DeYoung

In Christ, I am . . .

_____

_____

_____

_____

What brought me joy last week?

_____

_____

_____

_____

What might God be trying to speak to me through the events of the week?

_____

_____

_____

_____

How have I brought glory to God?

_____

_____

_____

_____

How does it feel when someone goes out of their way to bless me?

_____

_____

_____

_____

Challenge for Next Week

Go out of your way to bless someone.

What can you do to bless someone this week? Who in your life could benefit most from a spontaeous act of kindness? Is someone you know going through a crisis? How can you help them this week? Don't feel like you have to fix the situation. Just being there for them could be enough.

Or, you may know someone who needs encouragement. Go out of your way to show them how much they mean to you. That may mean spending time with them, a phone call to say you love them, or buying them a gift. Look for the act that will bless them the most. We each respond differently to acts of kindness, so look for the one that is right for them.

But don't stop with just one person. Look for ways to bless others all throughout the week. Begin noticing how many opportunites there are for you to positively impact the lives of those around you. You don't have to make big gestures. The smallest acts often have the greatest impact.

Use the "your notes" page this week to reflect on your experience of blessing others. Were you successful? How did it make you feel? What did you learn about yourself?

"O Lord, teach me how you want me to live! Then I will obey your commands. Make me wholeheartedly committed to you!"

Psalm 86:11

Date: _____

"Any discussion of how pain and suffering fit into God's scheme ultimately leads back to the cross."
—Philip Yancey

I am thankful for . . .

1. _____
2. _____
3. _____

God is calling me to be . . .

_____
_____
_____

I can serve God and others today by . . .

_____
_____
_____

My prayer for today is . . .

_____
_____
_____

🌙

Where or how did I see God at work today?

_____
_____
_____

What did I struggle with today that I want to overcome tomorrow?

_____
_____
_____

Your Notes

_____

_____

_____

_____

_____

_____

_____

_____

_____

_____

_____

_____

_____

_____

_____

_____

_____

_____

_____

_____

_____

_____

_____

_____

"Jesus answered, 'Neither this man nor his parents sinned, but he was born blind so that the acts of God may be revealed through what happens to him.'"

John 9:3

*"Faith is deliberate confidence in the character of God
whose ways you may not understand at the time."*
—*Oswald Chambers*

I am thankful for . . .

1. _____

2. _____

3. _____

God is calling me to be . . .

_____

_____

_____

I can serve God and others today by . . .

_____

_____

_____

My prayer for today is . . .

_____

_____

_____

Where or how did I see God at work today?

_____

_____

What did I struggle with today that I want to overcome tomorrow?

_____

_____

_____

Your Notes

_____
_____
_____
_____
_____
_____
_____
_____
_____
_____
_____
_____
_____
_____
_____
_____
_____
_____
_____
_____
_____
_____
_____

"Indeed, my plans are not like your plans, and my deeds are not like your deeds, for just as the sky is higher than the earth, so my deeds are superior to your deeds and my plans superior to your plans."

Isaiah 55:8-9

Date: _____ _____

*"Love always involves responsibility, and love always involves sacrifice.
And we do not really love Christ unless we are prepared
to face His task and to take up His Cross."*
—William Barclay

I am thankful for . . .

1. _____
2. _____
3. _____

God is calling me to be . . .

_____
_____
_____

I can serve God and others today by . . .

_____
_____
_____

My prayer for today is . . .

_____
_____
_____

☾

Where or how did I see God at work today?

_____
_____
_____

What did I struggle with today that I want to overcome tomorrow?

_____
_____
_____

Your Notes

_____

_____

_____

_____

_____

_____

_____

_____

_____

_____

_____

_____

_____

_____

_____

_____

_____

_____

_____

_____

_____

_____

_____

_____

"Then Jesus said to his disciples, 'If anyone wants to become my follower, he must deny himself, take up his cross, and follow me.'"

Matthew 16:24

Date: _____

"All the blessings we enjoy are Divine deposits, committed to our trust on this condition, that they should be dispensed for the benefit of our neighbors."
—John Calvin

I am thankful for . . .

1. _____
2. _____
3. _____

God is calling me to be . . .

_____
_____
_____

I can serve God and others today by . . .

_____
_____
_____

My prayer for today is . . .

_____
_____
_____

🌙

Where or how did I see God at work today?

_____
_____

What did I struggle with today that I want to overcome tomorrow?

_____
_____
_____

Your Notes

_____

_____

_____

_____

_____

_____

_____

_____

_____

_____

_____

_____

_____

_____

_____

_____

_____

_____

_____

_____

_____

_____

_____

_____

"From everyone who has been given much, much will be required, and from the one who has been entrusted with much, even more will be asked."

Luke 12:48

"The ultimate ground of faith and knowledge is confidence in God."
—Charles Hodge

I am thankful for . . .

1. _____
2. _____
3. _____

God is calling me to be . . .

_____
_____
_____

I can serve God and others today by . . .

_____
_____
_____

My prayer for today is . . .

_____
_____
_____

Where or how did I see God at work today?

_____
_____
_____

What did I struggle with today that I want to overcome tomorrow?

_____
_____
_____

Your Notes

_____

_____

_____

_____

_____

_____

_____

_____

_____

_____

_____

_____

_____

_____

_____

_____

_____

_____

_____

_____

_____

_____

"Trust in the Lord with all your heart, and do not rely on your own understanding. Acknowledge him in all your ways, and he will make your paths straight."

Proverbs 3:5-6

Date: _____ _____

"God grant me the serenity to accept the things I cannot change, the courage to change the things I can, and the wisdom to know the difference."
—Reinhold Niebuhr

✴

I am thankful for . . .

1. _____
2. _____
3. _____

God is calling me to be . . .

_____
_____
_____

I can serve God and others today by . . .

_____
_____
_____

My prayer for today is . . .

_____
_____
_____

☾

Where or how did I see God at work today?

_____
_____
_____

What did I struggle with today that I want to overcome tomorrow?

_____
_____
_____

Your Notes

_____

_____

_____

_____

_____

_____

_____

_____

_____

_____

_____

_____

_____

_____

_____

_____

_____

_____

_____

_____

_____

_____

_____

_____

_____

"My blessing is on those people who trust in me, who put their confidence in me. They will be like a tree planted near a stream whose roots spread out toward the water. It has nothing to fear when the heat comes. Its leaves are always green. It has no need to be concerned in a year of drought. It does not stop bearing fruit."

Jeremiah 17:7-8

Date: _____

Weekly Growth Check-In

"God's dream is the kingdom, that's already clear. But what is not always clear is that God's kingdom happens when human beings are empowered by God's Spirit to do God's kingdom work in the shape of a new community."
—Scot McKnight

In Christ, I am . . .

_____

_____

_____

What brought me joy last week?

_____

_____

What might God be trying to speak to me through the events of the week?

_____

_____

How have I brought glory to God?

_____

_____

How have I added value to someone else's life?

_____

_____

In what area of my life do I wish I were more like Christ?

_____

_____

_____

Challenge

Prioritize your time for what's really important to you.

If you are struggling to find time to journal or practice other spiritual disciplines, ask yourself "why?" Evaluate what's important in your life and see if there are ways you can make time to spend with God practicing spiritual growth.

1. Start by listing out your daily routine.
2. Decide if all those activities are helping you accomplish your purpose and cut out the ones that aren't.
3. Look for additional time to set aside and dedicate to spending with God. You may need to wake up 15 minutes earlier in the morning, or maybe cut out some TV or social media time.

Don't feel like you have to set aside a full hour. Making small incremental changes is the best way to ensure success when trying to establish a new habit or routine.

Use the "your notes" page to reflect on your experience of using the Daily Growth Journal. How has it helped you grow in your walk with Christ?

"The kingdom of heaven is like a mustard seed that a man took and sowed in his field. It is the smallest of all the seeds, but when it has grown it is the greatest garden plant and becomes a tree, so that the wild birds come and nest in its branches."

Matthew 13:31-32

Date: _____ _____

"In the Church of Jesus Christ there can and should be no non-theologians."
—*Karl Barth*

I am thankful for . . .

1. _____
2. _____
3. _____

God is calling me to be . . .

_____

_____

_____

I can serve God and others today by . . .

_____

_____

_____

My prayer for today is . . .

_____

_____

_____

Where or how did I see God at work today?

_____

_____

What did I struggle with today that I want to overcome tomorrow?

_____

_____

_____

Your Notes

_____

_____

_____

_____

_____

_____

_____

_____

_____

_____

_____

_____

_____

_____

_____

_____

_____

_____

_____

_____

_____

_____

_____

"Therefore we must progress beyond the elementary instructions about Christ and move on to maturity, not laying this foundation again: repentance from dead works and faith in God, teaching about baptisms, laying on of hands, resurrection of the dead, and eternal judgment. And this is what we intend to do, if God permits."

Hebrews 6:1-3

"Only a very few can be learned, but all can be Christian, all can be devout, and—I shall boldly add—all can be theologians."
—Desiderius Erasmus

I am thankful for . . .

1. _____
2. _____
3. _____

God is calling me to be . . .

_____
_____
_____

I can serve God and others today by . . .

_____
_____
_____

My prayer for today is . . .

_____
_____
_____

🌙

Where or how did I see God at work today?

_____
_____
_____

What did I struggle with today that I want to overcome tomorrow?

_____
_____
_____

Your Notes

_____
_____
_____
_____
_____
_____
_____
_____
_____
_____
_____
_____
_____
_____
_____
_____
_____
_____
_____
_____
_____
_____
_____
_____

"Do not be conformed to this present world, but be transformed by the renewing of your mind, so that you may test and approve what is the will of God—what is good and well-pleasing and perfect."

Romans 12:2

Date: _____   _____

"Theological formation is the gradual and often painful discovery of God's incomprehensibility. You can be competent in many things, but you cannot be competent in God."
—Henri J.M. Nouwen

I am thankful for . . .

1. _____
2. _____
3. _____

God is calling me to be . . .

_____
_____
_____

I can serve God and others today by . . .

_____
_____
_____

My prayer for today is . . .

_____
_____
_____

Where or how did I see God at work today?

_____
_____

What did I struggle with today that I want to overcome tomorrow?

_____
_____
_____

Your Notes

_____

_____

_____

_____

_____

_____

_____

_____

_____

_____

_____

_____

_____

_____

_____

_____

_____

_____

_____

_____

_____

_____

_____

_____

"For who has known the mind of the Lord, so as to advise him?
But we have the mind of Christ."

1 Corinthians 2:16

"How many hours are there in a mile? Is yellow square or round? Probably half the questions we ask—half our great theological and metaphysical problems—are like that."
—C.S. Lewis

I am thankful for . . .

1. _____
2. _____
3. _____

God is calling me to be . . .

_____
_____
_____

I can serve God and others today by . . .

_____
_____
_____

My prayer for today is . . .

_____
_____
_____

🌙

Where or how did I see God at work today?

_____
_____
_____

What did I struggle with today that I want to overcome tomorrow?

_____
_____
_____

Your Notes

_____
_____
_____
_____
_____
_____
_____
_____
_____
_____
_____
_____
_____
_____
_____
_____
_____
_____
_____
_____
_____
_____
_____
_____

"Oh, the depth of the riches and wisdom and knowledge of God! How unsearchable are his judgments and how fathomless his ways!"

Romans 11:33

"The goal of theology is not to figure out God, but to accept what He's revealed through Jesus' life, death, and resurrection."
—Chris Lamberth

I am thankful for . . .

1. _____

2. _____

3. _____

God is calling me to be . . .

_____

_____

_____

I can serve God and others today by . . .

_____

_____

_____

My prayer for today is . . .

_____

_____

_____

☾

Where or how did I see God at work today?

_____

_____

_____

What did I struggle with today that I want to overcome tomorrow?

_____

_____

_____

Your Notes

_____
_____
_____
_____
_____
_____
_____
_____
_____
_____
_____
_____
_____
_____
_____
_____
_____
_____
_____
_____
_____
_____
_____
_____

"For this is the way God loved the world: He gave his one and only Son, so that everyone who believes in him will not perish but have eternal life."

John 3:16

Date: _____ |⊢

*"He that has doctrinal knowledge and speculation only,
without affection, never is engaged in the business of religion."*
—Jonathan Edwards

☀

I am thankful for . . .

1. _____
2. _____
3. _____

God is calling me to be . . .

_____
_____
_____

I can serve God and others today by . . .

_____
_____
_____

My prayer for today is . . .

_____
_____
_____

☾

Where or how did I see God at work today?

_____
_____

What did I struggle with today that I want to overcome tomorrow?

_____
_____
_____

Your Notes

_____

_____

_____

_____

_____

_____

_____

_____

_____

_____

_____

_____

_____

_____

_____

_____

_____

_____

_____

_____

_____

_____

_____

"If a brother or sister is poorly clothed and lacks daily food, and one of you says to them, 'Go in peace, keep warm and eat well,' but you do not give them what the body needs, what good is it? So also faith, if it does not have works, is dead being by itself."

James 2:15-17

Date: _____ _____

Weekly Growth Check-In

"The significance of the crucifixion is not only what God does for us; consistently throughout the New Testament the crucifixion is portrayed as the pattern that we are to follow. It is a model of social behavior toward the other as well as a statement about what God has done for us. "
—Miroslav Volf

In Christ, I am . . .

_____

_____

_____

What brought me joy last week?

_____

_____

What might God be trying to speak to me through the events of the week?

_____

_____

How have I brought glory to God?

_____

_____

How have I added value to someone else's life?

_____

_____

How could my current prayer life be improved?

_____

_____

_____

Challenge

Spend some extra time this week in prayer.

If you already have a prayer routine, then try adding an additional 15-30 minutes of prayer at a different time in the day. Spending additional time in prayer when it's out of your normal routine can really enhance your awareness of God's presence. We can get so caught up with the daily grind that often we don't listen for the voice the Lord throughout the day. Interrupting your day to pray causes you to be especially mindful of Him.

If you don't have a normal prayer life, don't feel pressured to start with a large amount of time. Choose a time of day that works best for you and begin with just 15-30 minutes. Getting in the routine is more important than how long you actually pray. Focus on *quality* instead of *quantity*.

Use the "your notes" page to reflect on your prayer time this week. What have you been praying about? How has this extra time of prayer affected your day?

"You were taught with reference to your former way of life to lay aside the old man who is being corrupted in accordance with deceitful desires, to be renewed in the spirit of your mind, and to put on the new man who has been created in God's image—in righteousness and holiness that comes from truth."

Ephesians 4:22-24

Date:

"The success of our living ready is dependent on our giving ourselves in prayer."
—E. M. Bounds

I am thankful for . . .

1. _____
2. _____
3. _____

God is calling me to be . . .

_____
_____
_____

I can serve God and others today by . . .

_____
_____
_____

My prayer for today is . . .

_____
_____
_____

Where or how did I see God at work today?

_____
_____
_____

What did I struggle with today that I want to overcome tomorrow?

_____
_____
_____

Your Notes

_____
_____
_____
_____
_____
_____
_____
_____
_____
_____
_____
_____
_____
_____
_____
_____
_____
_____
_____
_____
_____
_____
_____
_____

"With every prayer and petition, pray at all times in the Spirit, and to this end be alert, with all perseverance and requests for all the saints."

Ephesians 6:18

"Nothing changes until you find new ways
of dealing with persistent dissatisfaction."
—Dan Rockwell

I am thankful for . . .

1. _____
2. _____
3. _____

God is calling me to be . . .

_____
_____
_____

I can serve God and others today by . . .

_____
_____
_____

My prayer for today is . . .

_____
_____
_____

Where or how did I see God at work today?

_____
_____
_____

What did I struggle with today that I want to overcome tomorrow?

_____
_____
_____

Your Notes

_____

_____

_____

_____

_____

_____

_____

_____

_____

_____

_____

_____

_____

_____

_____

_____

_____

_____

_____

_____

_____

_____

_____

"The godly cry out and the Lord hears;he saves them from all their troubles.
The Lord is near the brokenhearted; he delivers those who are discouraged."

Psalm 34:17-18

Date: _____ _____

"To pray without ceasing is to join one's prayer with one's daily work."
—Origen

I am thankful for . . .

1. _____
2. _____
3. _____

God is calling me to be . . .

_____
_____
_____

I can serve God and others today by . . .

_____
_____
_____

My prayer for today is . . .

_____
_____
_____

🌙

Where or how did I see God at work today?

_____
_____

What did I struggle with today that I want to overcome tomorrow?

_____
_____
_____

Your Notes

_____

_____

_____

_____

_____

_____

_____

_____

_____

_____

_____

_____

_____

_____

_____

_____

_____

_____

_____

_____

_____

_____

"So pray this way: Our Father in heaven, may your name be honored, may your kingdom come, may your will be done on earth as it is in heaven. Give us today our daily bread, and forgive us our debts, as we ourselves have forgiven our debtors. And do not lead us into temptation, but deliver us from the evil one."

Matthew 6:9-13

Date: _____ _____

"Prayer will make a man cease from sin,
or sin will entice a man to cease from prayer."
—John Bunyan

I am thankful for . . .

1. _____
2. _____
3. _____

God is calling me to be . . .

_____
_____
_____

I can serve God and others today by . . .

_____
_____
_____

My prayer for today is . . .

_____
_____
_____

☾

Where or how did I see God at work today?

_____
_____
_____

What did I struggle with today that I want to overcome tomorrow?

_____
_____
_____

Your Notes

_____

_____

_____

_____

_____

_____

_____

_____

_____

_____

_____

_____

_____

_____

_____

_____

_____

_____

_____

_____

_____

_____

_____

_____

_____

_____

"With every prayer and petition, pray at all times in the Spirit, and to this end be alert, with all perseverance and requests for all the saints."

Ephesians 6:18

Date:

"If we knew what God knows, we would ask exactly for what he gives."
—*Tim Keller*

I am thankful for . . .

1. _____
2. _____
3. _____

God is calling me to be . . .

_____
_____
_____

I can serve God and others today by . . .

_____
_____
_____

My prayer for today is . . .

_____
_____
_____

Where or how did I see God at work today?

_____
_____

What did I struggle with today that I want to overcome tomorrow?

_____
_____
_____

Your Notes

_____

_____

_____

_____

_____

_____

_____

_____

_____

_____

_____

_____

_____

_____

_____

_____

_____

_____

_____

_____

_____

_____

_____

_____

_____

_____

"If you then, although you are evil, know how to give good gifts to your children, how much more will your Father in heaven give good gifts to those who ask him!"

Matthew 7:11

Date: _____ _____

"To be a Christian without prayer is no more possible
than to be alive without breathing."
—Martin Luther

I am thankful for . . .

1. _____
2. _____
3. _____

God is calling me to be . . .

_____

_____

_____

I can serve God and others today by . . .

_____

_____

_____

My prayer for today is . . .

_____

_____

_____

☾

Where or how did I see God at work today?

_____

_____

What did I struggle with today that I want to overcome tomorrow?

_____

_____

_____

Your Notes

_____
_____
_____
_____
_____
_____
_____
_____
_____
_____
_____
_____
_____
_____
_____
_____
_____
_____
_____
_____
_____
_____
_____
_____

"Yet Jesus himself frequently withdrew to the wilderness and prayed."

Luke 5:16

Weekly Growth Check-In

"He who was not legalist at any other point, and who was ready without hesitation to pardon prostitutes and disreputable people, was nonetheless extremely strict upon one point: 'only one who practices grace can receive grace.'"
—John Howard Yoder

In Christ, I am . . .

_____

_____

_____

What brought me joy last week?

_____

_____

What might God be trying to speak to me through the events of the week?

_____

_____

How have I brought glory to God?

_____

_____

How have I added value to someone else's life?

_____

_____

What is one bad habit I wish I could break? Why?

_____

_____

_____

Challenge

Break a bad habit and replace it with a good one.

Bad habits are more successfully broken when they're replaced with good ones. We form bad habits in response to stress and other negative stimuli. Bad habits are nearly impossible to break unless we change the underlying reason why we started them in the first place. Replacing a bad habit with a beneficial one helps ensure success.

Motivate yourself to break this habit by focusing on what you'll gain from the new one, not on what you're losing. Write down what you'll get from overcoming this bad habit and post it on your bathroom mirror, your refrigerator, and your office wall to constantly remind yourself of the prize in front of you.

Use the "your notes" page this week to track your progress and journal about your desire to implement this new behavior into your life. You can answer these questions to help keep you motivated: How will this new habit make your life better? How will it impact those around you? How will it glorify God?

"Blessed are the merciful, for they will be shown mercy."

Matthew 5:7

Date: _____ _____

"Believers should acknowledge and wrestle with doubts ... It is no longer
sufficient to hold beliefs just because you inherited them."
—Timothy Keller

I am thankful for . . .

1. _____
2. _____
3. _____

God is calling me to be . . .

_____
_____
_____

I can serve God and others today by . . .

_____
_____
_____

My prayer for today is . . .

_____
_____
_____

Where or how did I see God at work today?

_____
_____
_____

What did I struggle with today that I want to overcome tomorrow?

_____
_____
_____

Your Notes

_____

_____

_____

_____

_____

_____

_____

_____

_____

_____

_____

_____

_____

_____

_____

_____

_____

_____

_____

_____

_____

"So then, my dear friends, just as you have always obeyed, not only in my presence but even more in my absence, continue working out your salvation with awe and reverence, for the one bringing forth in you both the desire and the effort—for the sake of his good pleasure—is God."

Philippians 2:12-13

Date: _____ ⊢_____

"The peace of the celestial city is the perfectly ordered and harmonious enjoyment of God, and of one another in God."
—Augustine of Hippo

☀

I am thankful for . . .

1. _____
2. _____
3. _____

God is calling me to be . . .

_____
_____
_____

I can serve God and others today by . . .

_____
_____
_____

My prayer for today is . . .

_____
_____
_____

☾

Where or how did I see God at work today?

_____
_____

What did I struggle with today that I want to overcome tomorrow?

_____
_____
_____

Your Notes

_____

_____

_____

_____

_____

_____

_____

_____

_____

_____

_____

_____

_____

_____

_____

_____

_____

_____

_____

_____

_____

_____

_____

"The kingdom of heaven is like a treasure, hidden in a field, that a person found and hid. Then because of joy he went and sold all that he had and bought that field."

Matthew 13:44

Date:

"*Sovereignty means exercising kingly power. We use the word in relation to God meaning that there is absolutely nothing that he does not control.*"
—*Graeme Goldsworthy*

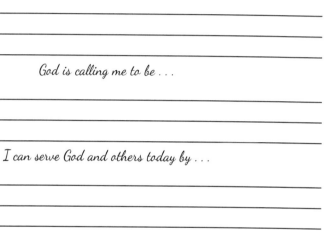

I am thankful for . . .

1. _____
2. _____
3. _____

God is calling me to be . . .

_____
_____
_____

I can serve God and others today by . . .

_____
_____
_____

My prayer for today is . . .

_____
_____
_____

Where or how did I see God at work today?

_____
_____

What did I struggle with today that I want to overcome tomorrow?

_____
_____
_____

Your Notes

_____
_____
_____
_____
_____
_____
_____
_____
_____
_____
_____
_____
_____
_____
_____
_____
_____
_____
_____
_____
_____
_____
_____
_____
_____

"Yes, I know the Lord is great, and our Lord is superior to all gods. He does whatever he pleases in heaven and on earth, in the seas and all the ocean depths."

Psalm 135:5-6

"The cross is not a detour or a hurdle on the way to the kingdom, nor is it even the way to the kingdom; it is the kingdom come."
—John Howard Yoder

I am thankful for . . .

1. _____
2. _____
3. _____

God is calling me to be . . .

_____
_____
_____

I can serve God and others today by . . .

_____
_____
_____

My prayer for today is . . .

_____
_____
_____

☾

Where or how did I see God at work today?

_____
_____
_____

What did I struggle with today that I want to overcome tomorrow?

_____
_____
_____

Your Notes

_____

_____

_____

_____

_____

_____

_____

_____

_____

_____

_____

_____

_____

_____

_____

_____

_____

_____

_____

_____

_____

_____

_____

_____

_____

"For the message about the cross is foolishness to those who are perishing, but to us who are being saved it is the power of God."

1 Corinthians 1:18

Date: _____ _____

"Jesus Christ is the beginning, the middle, and the end of all. In the Gospels he walks in human form upon the earth, and accomplishes the work of redemption."
—Philip Schaff

I am thankful for . . .

1. _____
2. _____
3. _____

God is calling me to be . . .

_____

_____

_____

I can serve God and others today by . . .

_____

_____

_____

My prayer for today is . . .

_____

_____

_____

Where or how did I see God at work today?

_____

_____

_____

What did I struggle with today that I want to overcome tomorrow?

_____

_____

_____

Your Notes

_____
_____
_____
_____
_____
_____
_____
_____
_____
_____
_____
_____
_____
_____
_____
_____
_____
_____
_____
_____
_____
_____
_____

"I am the Alpha and the Omega, the first and the last, the beginning and the end!"

Revelation 22:13

Date: _____ _____

*"How quickly we forget God's great deliverances in our lives.
How easily we take for granted the miracles he performed in our past."
—David Wilkerson*

I am thankful for . . .

1. _____
2. _____
3. _____

God is calling me to be . . .

_____
_____
_____

I can serve God and others today by . . .

_____
_____
_____

My prayer for today is . . .

_____
_____
_____

Where or how did I see God at work today?

_____
_____

What did I struggle with today that I want to overcome tomorrow?

_____
_____
_____

Your Notes

_____
_____
_____
_____
_____
_____
_____
_____
_____
_____
_____
_____
_____
_____
_____
_____
_____
_____
_____
_____
_____
_____

Praise the Lord, O my soul! With all that is within me, praise his holy name!
Praise the Lord, O my soul! Do not forget all his kind deeds! He is the one
who forgives all your sins, who heals all your diseases, who delivers your life
from the Pit, who crowns you with his loyal love and compassion, who satisfies
your life with good things, so your youth is renewed like an eagle's.

Psalm 103:1-5

Weekly Growth Check-In

"A knowledge of the Bible is essential to a rich and meaningful life."
—Billy Graham

In Christ, I am . . .

_____

_____

_____

What brought me joy last week?

_____

_____

_____

What might God be trying to speak to me through the events of the week?

_____

_____

_____

How have I brought glory to God?

_____

_____

_____

How have I added value to someone else's life?

_____

_____

_____

What has my experience been like with reading the Bible?

_____

_____

_____

Challenge

Set aside some time this week to read an entire book of the Bible.

The New Testament has many short books that can easily be read through in one sitting. Our perspective changes when we read Scripture as a whole instead of one chapter at a time.

Write down any questions that come to mind as you read. They could be about people mentioned, the context, the culture, or how you can better understand what the text means and how it applies to your life.

Reading the Bible is only beneficial if you understand what you're reading. It can be helpful to read along with a commentary. A great place to start is with online commentaries on some of the popular Bible reading websites.

Use the "your notes" page this week to write down your questions as you read the Bible. Search for the answers using commentaries, books, your pastor, or your friends. Then journal about your experience of digging deeper into Scripture.

"This law scroll must not leave your lips! You must memorize it day and night so you can carefully obey all that is written in it. Then you will prosper and be successful."

Joshua 1:8

Date: _____ _____

"Jesus and the cross provide the central key to the whole meaning of human history within the plan of God."
—Christopher Wright

☀

I am thankful for . . .

1. _____
2. _____
3. _____

God is calling me to be . . .

_____
_____
_____

I can serve God and others today by . . .

_____
_____
_____

My prayer for today is . . .

_____
_____
_____

☾

Where or how did I see God at work today?

_____
_____
_____

What did I struggle with today that I want to overcome tomorrow?

_____
_____
_____

Your Notes

_____

_____

_____

_____

_____

_____

_____

_____

_____

_____

_____

_____

_____

_____

_____

_____

_____

_____

_____

_____

_____

_____

_____

"Then he said to them, 'These are my words that I spoke to you while I was still with you, that everything written about me in the law of Moses and the prophets and the psalms must be fulfilled.'"

Luke 24:44

"True humility is not thinking less of yourself, but thinking of yourself less."
—C.S. Lewis

I am thankful for . . .

1. _____
2. _____
3. _____

God is calling me to be . . .

_____
_____
_____

I can serve God and others today by . . .

_____
_____
_____

My prayer for today is . . .

_____
_____
_____

Where or how did I see God at work today?

_____
_____
_____

What did I struggle with today that I want to overcome tomorrow?

_____
_____
_____

Your Notes

"Pride goes before destruction, and a haughty spirit before a fall."

Proverbs 16:18

"Original sin is that thing about man which makes him capable of conceiving of his own perfection and incapable of achieving it."
—Reinhold Niebuhr

I am thankful for . . .

1. _____
2. _____
3. _____

God is calling me to be . . .

_____
_____
_____

I can serve God and others today by . . .

_____
_____
_____

My prayer for today is . . .

_____
_____
_____

Where or how did I see God at work today?

_____
_____
_____

What did I struggle with today that I want to overcome tomorrow?

_____
_____
_____

Your Notes

_____

_____

_____

_____

_____

_____

_____

_____

_____

_____

_____

_____

_____

_____

_____

_____

_____

_____

_____

_____

_____

_____

_____

"Now we know that whatever the law says, it says to those who are under the law, so that every mouth may be silenced and the whole world may be held accountable to God. For no one is declared righteous before him by the works of the law, for through the law comes the knowledge of sin."

Romans 3:19-20

"It is not good for us to trust in our merits, in our virtues or our righteousness; but only in God's free pardon, as given us through faith in Jesus Christ."
—*John Wycliffe*

I am thankful for . . .

1. _____
2. _____
3. _____

God is calling me to be . . .

_____
_____
_____

I can serve God and others today by . . .

_____
_____
_____

My prayer for today is . . .

_____
_____
_____

Where or how did I see God at work today?

_____
_____

What did I struggle with today that I want to overcome tomorrow?

_____
_____
_____

Your Notes

_____

_____

_____

_____

_____

_____

_____

_____

_____

_____

_____

_____

_____

_____

_____

_____

_____

_____

_____

_____

_____

_____

_____

"For by grace you are saved through faith, and this is not from yourselves, it is the gift of God; it is not from works, so that no one can boast. For we are his workmanship, having been created in Christ Jesus for good works that God prepared beforehand so we may do them."

Ephesians 2:8-10

Date: _____ _____

"*We sinned for no reason but an incomprehensible lack of love, and He saved us for no reason but an incomprehensible excess of love.*"
—*Peter Kreeft*

I am thankful for . . .

1. _____
2. _____
3. _____

God is calling me to be . . .

_____

_____

_____

I can serve God and others today by . . .

_____

_____

_____

My prayer for today is . . .

_____

_____

_____

Where or how did I see God at work today?

_____

_____

_____

What did I struggle with today that I want to overcome tomorrow?

_____

_____

_____

Your Notes

_____
_____
_____
_____
_____
_____
_____
_____
_____
_____
_____
_____
_____
_____
_____
_____
_____
_____
_____
_____
_____
_____
_____
_____
_____

"But God demonstrates his own love for us, in that while we were still sinners, Christ died for us."

Romans 5:8

"I take for granted that Christian revelation is the only full revelation and that the fullness of Christian revelation resides in the essential fact of the Incarnation ... The division between those who accept, and those who deny, Christian revelation I take to be the most profound division between human beings."
—T.S. Eliot

I am thankful for . . .

1. _____
2. _____
3. _____

God is calling me to be . . .

_____
_____
_____

I can serve God and others today by . . .

_____
_____
_____

My prayer for today is . . .

_____
_____
_____

☾

Where or how did I see God at work today?

_____
_____
_____

What did I struggle with today that I want to overcome tomorrow?

_____
_____
_____

Your Notes

_____

_____

_____

_____

_____

_____

_____

_____

_____

_____

_____

_____

_____

_____

_____

_____

_____

_____

_____

_____

_____

_____

_____

_____

"In the beginning was the Word, and the Word was with God, and the Word was fully God. The Word was with God in the beginning. All things were created by him, and apart from him not one thing was created that has been created."

John 1:1-3

Weekly Growth Check-In

*"The spirit of Christ is the spirit of missions. The nearer we get to Him,
the more intensely missionary we become."*
—Henry Martyn

In Christ, I am . . .

_____

_____

_____

What brought me joy last week?

_____

_____

What might God be trying to speak to me through the events of the week?

_____

_____

_____

How have I brought glory to God?

_____

_____

_____

How have I added value to someone else's life?

_____

_____

What do I feel is life's purpose?

_____

_____

_____

Challenge

Evaluate your commitments to determine if you are working toward your life purpose.

Consider cutting back on activities that aren't essential to what God has called you to. Write down your life goals and determine if you're currently working towards them.

Overcommitting to please others drains your energy and keeps you from finding fulfillment in your own life. Make a list of the things getting in the way of what's most important to you. Then write what you believe to be the root cause of each distraction you listed.

Use the "your notes" page this week to write down life goals you hope to accomplish. Then answer the following: Why do you want to accomplish these goals? Are your goals about serving others or yourself? Are you doing all you can to achieve your goals?

"You did not choose me, but I chose you and appointed you to go and bear fruit, fruit that remains, so that whatever you ask the Father in my name he will give you."

John 15:16

Date: _____

"Our hope in life beyond death is a hope made possible, not by some general sentimental belief in life after death, but by our participation in the life of Christ."
—Stanley Hauerwas

I am thankful for . . .

1. _____
2. _____
3. _____

God is calling me to be . . .

_____
_____
_____

I can serve God and others today by . . .

_____
_____
_____

My prayer for today is . . .

_____
_____
_____

Where or how did I see God at work today?

_____
_____
_____

What did I struggle with today that I want to overcome tomorrow?

_____
_____
_____

Your Notes

_____
_____
_____
_____
_____
_____
_____
_____
_____
_____
_____
_____
_____
_____
_____
_____
_____
_____
_____
_____
_____
_____

"For if someone merely listens to the message and does not live it out, he is like someone who gazes at his own face in a mirror."

James 1:23

Date: _____ |—————————————

"The God who walks the paths of history through the pages of the Bible pins a mission statement to every signpost on the way."
—Christopher J.H. Wright

I am thankful for . . .

1. _____

2. _____

3. _____

God is calling me to be . . .

_____

_____

_____

I can serve God and others today by . . .

_____

_____

_____

My prayer for today is . . .

_____

_____

_____

🌙

Where or how did I see God at work today?

_____

_____

_____

What did I struggle with today that I want to overcome tomorrow?

_____

_____

_____

Your Notes

_____

_____

_____

_____

_____

_____

_____

_____

_____

_____

_____

_____

_____

_____

_____

_____

_____

_____

_____

_____

_____

_____

_____

"Tell the nations about his splendor! Tell all the nations about his amazing deeds!"

Psalm 96:3

"The point of your life is to point to Him. Whatever you are doing,
God wants to be glorified, because this whole thing is His."
—*Francis Chan*

I am thankful for . . .

1. _____
2. _____
3. _____

God is calling me to be . . .

_____
_____
_____

I can serve God and others today by . . .

_____
_____
_____

My prayer for today is . . .

_____
_____
_____

Where or how did I see God at work today?

_____
_____

What did I struggle with today that I want to overcome tomorrow?

_____
_____
_____

Your Notes

_____

"For you were bought at a price. Therefore glorify God with your body."

1 Corinthians 6:20

"Disciple making is not a call for others to come to us to hear the gospel but a command for us to go to others to share the gospel."
—David Platt

I am thankful for . . .

1. _____
2. _____
3. _____

God is calling me to be . . .

_____
_____
_____

I can serve God and others today by . . .

_____
_____
_____

My prayer for today is . . .

_____
_____
_____

Where or how did I see God at work today?

_____
_____

What did I struggle with today that I want to overcome tomorrow?

_____
_____
_____

Your Notes

_____

_____

_____

_____

_____

_____

_____

_____

_____

_____

_____

_____

_____

_____

_____

_____

_____

_____

_____

_____

_____

_____

_____

_____

_____

_____

"He said to them, 'Go into all the world and preach the gospel to every creature.'"

Mark 16:15

Date: _____ _____

"The whole point of the kingdom of God is Jesus has come to bear witness to the true truth, which is nonviolent. When God wants to take charge of the world, he doesn't send in the tanks. He sends in the poor and the meek."
—N. T. Wright

I am thankful for . . .

1. _____
2. _____
3. _____

God is calling me to be . . .

_____
_____
_____

I can serve God and others today by . . .

_____
_____
_____

My prayer for today is . . .

_____
_____
_____

☾

Where or how did I see God at work today?

_____
_____

What did I struggle with today that I want to overcome tomorrow?

_____
_____
_____

Your Notes

_____

_____

_____

_____

_____

_____

_____

_____

_____

_____

_____

_____

_____

_____

_____

_____

_____

_____

_____

_____

_____

_____

_____

_____

"Blessed are the poor in spirit, for the kingdom of heaven belongs to them."

Matthew 5:3

Date: _____ _____

"We are under God's power, and we can do nothing but by the power of God, and woe shall hereafter be to us if we abuse this power. "
—John Wycliffe

I am thankful for . . .

1. _____
2. _____
3. _____

God is calling me to be . . .

_____
_____
_____

I can serve God and others today by . . .

_____
_____
_____

My prayer for today is . . .

_____
_____
_____

☽

Where or how did I see God at work today?

_____
_____
_____

What did I struggle with today that I want to overcome tomorrow?

_____
_____
_____

Your Notes

_____

_____

_____

_____

_____

_____

_____

_____

_____

_____

_____

_____

_____

_____

_____

_____

_____

_____

_____

_____

_____

_____

_____

_____

"Those who are in the flesh cannot please God. You, however, are not in the flesh but in the Spirit, if indeed the Spirit of God lives in you. Now if anyone does not have the Spirit of Christ, this person does not belong to him. But if Christ is in you, your body is dead because of sin, but the Spirit is your life because of righteousness."

Romans 8:8-10

Weekly Growth Check-In

"When we put our problems in God's hands, he puts his peace in our hearts."
—Anonymous

In Christ, I am . . .

_____

_____

What brought me joy last week?

_____

_____

What might God be trying to speak to me through the events of the week?

_____

_____

How have I brought glory to God?

_____

_____

How have I added value to someone else's life?

_____

_____

*How have I become more aware of God's presence
in my life since I began using this journal?*

_____

_____

Challenge

Practice mindfulness in an additional area of your life.

Practicing mindfulness must be intentional. You're already practicing mindfulness when you journal, but this week choose one task below and practice it as well through the week.

- *Complain less.* Every time you complain, write down three things you're thankful for. Hold yourself accountable by telling a friend what you're doing and have them check in with you each day.
- *Reduce road rage.* Instead of getting angry and hurling insults while on the road, try seeing them as children of God. Love and bless them instead.
- *Meditate for 20 minutes each day.* Find a place to quietly sit and meditate on God's grace in your life.
- You could also spend this week focusing on breaking a bad habit if you're still having trouble from a couple of weeks ago.

The point of this should be to focus on God's presence and grace. How does God's Spirit affect your daily routine?

Use the "your notes" page this week to reflect on your mindfulness practice. Have you been more aware of God's presence in your life this week? What has been the biggest change this week?

"Come to me, all you who are weary and burdened, and I will give you rest. Take my yoke on you and learn from me, because I am gentle and humble in heart, and you will find rest for your souls."

Matthew 11:28-29

Date: _____ |_____

"Beware of anything that competes with your loyalty to Jesus Christ. The greatest competitor of true devotion to Jesus is the service we do for Him. It is easier to serve than to pour out our lives completely for Him."
—*Oswald Chambers*

I am thankful for . . .

1. _____
2. _____
3. _____

God is calling me to be . . .

_____
_____
_____

I can serve God and others today by . . .

_____
_____
_____

My prayer for today is . . .

_____
_____
_____

Where or how did I see God at work today?

_____
_____
_____

What did I struggle with today that I want to overcome tomorrow?

_____
_____
_____

Your Notes

_____

_____

_____

_____

_____

_____

_____

_____

_____

_____

_____

_____

_____

_____

_____

_____

_____

_____

_____

_____

_____

_____

_____

_____

_____

_____

"Not everyone who says to me, 'Lord, Lord,' will enter into the kingdom of heaven—only the one who does the will of my Father in heaven. On that day, many will say to me, 'Lord, Lord, didn't we prophesy in your name, and in your name cast out demons and do many powerful deeds?' Then I will declare to them, 'I never knew you. Go away from me, you lawbreakers!'"

Matthew 7:21-23

"Christian meditation, very simply, is the ability to hear God's voice and obey his word."
—Richard Foster

I am thankful for . . .

1. _____
2. _____
3. _____

God is calling me to be . . .

_____
_____
_____

I can serve God and others today by . . .

_____
_____
_____

My prayer for today is . . .

_____
_____
_____

🌙

Where or how did I see God at work today?

_____
_____

What did I struggle with today that I want to overcome tomorrow?

_____
_____
_____

Your Notes

_____

_____

_____

_____

_____

_____

_____

_____

_____

_____

_____

_____

_____

_____

_____

_____

_____

_____

_____

_____

_____

_____

_____

_____

_____

"I will listen to what God the Lord says. For he will make peace with his people, his faithful followers. Yet they must not return to their foolish ways."

Psalm 85:8

Date: _____ _____

"Life is 10% what happens to me and 90% how I react to it."
—Charles R. Swindoll

I am thankful for . . .

1. _____
2. _____
3. _____

God is calling me to be . . .

_____
_____
_____

I can serve God and others today by . . .

_____
_____
_____

My prayer for today is . . .

_____
_____
_____

Where or how did I see God at work today?

_____
_____

What did I struggle with today that I want to overcome tomorrow?

_____
_____
_____

Your Notes

_____

_____

_____

_____

_____

_____

_____

_____

_____

_____

_____

_____

_____

_____

_____

_____

_____

_____

_____

_____

_____

_____

_____

_____

_____

"When the fig tree does not bud, and there are no grapes on the vines; when the olive trees do not produce, and the fields yield no crops; when the sheep disappear from the pen, and there are no cattle in the stalls, I will rejoice because of the Lord; I will be happy because of the God who delivers me!"

Habakkuk 3:17-18

Date: _____ _____

"An unexamined life is not worth living."
—Socrates

I am thankful for . . .

1. _____
2. _____
3. _____

God is calling me to be . . .

_____

_____

_____

I can serve God and others today by . . .

_____

_____

_____

My prayer for today is . . .

_____

_____

_____

☾

Where or how did I see God at work today?

_____

_____

_____

What did I struggle with today that I want to overcome tomorrow?

_____

_____

_____

Your Notes

_____
_____
_____
_____
_____
_____
_____
_____
_____
_____
_____
_____
_____
_____
_____
_____
_____
_____
_____
_____
_____
_____
_____

"For the word of God is living and active and sharper than any double-edged sword, piercing even to the point of dividing soul from spirit, and joints from marrow; it is able to judge the desires and thoughts of the heart."

Hebrews 4:12

Date: _____ |————————————————

"*Mastering our emotions has nothing to do with asceticism or repression, for the purpose is not to break the emotions or deny them but to 'break in' the emotions, making them teachable because they are tamed.*"
—Os Guinness

I am thankful for . . .

1. _____
2. _____
3. _____

God is calling me to be . . .

_____
_____
_____

I can serve God and others today by . . .

_____
_____
_____

My prayer for today is . . .

_____
_____
_____

Where or how did I see God at work today?

_____
_____
_____

What did I struggle with today that I want to overcome tomorrow?

_____
_____
_____

Your Notes

_____

_____

_____

_____

_____

_____

_____

_____

_____

_____

_____

_____

_____

_____

_____

_____

_____

_____

_____

_____

_____

_____

_____

_____

"Better to be slow to anger than to be a mighty warrior, and one who controls his temper is better than one who captures a city."

Proverbs 16:32

Date: _____ ⊢_____

"Joy is the simplest form of gratitude."
—Karl Barth

I am thankful for . . .

1. _____
2. _____
3. _____

God is calling me to be . . .

_____
_____
_____

I can serve God and others today by . . .

_____
_____
_____

My prayer for today is . . .

_____
_____
_____

🌙

Where or how did I see God at work today?

_____
_____

What did I struggle with today that I want to overcome tomorrow?

_____
_____
_____

Your Notes

_____
_____
_____
_____
_____
_____
_____
_____
_____
_____
_____
_____
_____
_____
_____
_____
_____
_____
_____
_____
_____
_____
_____
_____
_____

"Always rejoice, constantly pray, in everything give thanks. For this is God's will for you in Christ Jesus."

1 Thessalonians 5:16-18

Weekly Growth Check-In

"The custom of sinning takes away the sense of it,
the course of the world takes away the shame of it."
—John Owen

In Christ, I am . . .

_____

_____

_____

What brought me joy last week?

_____

_____

What might God be trying to speak to me through the events of the week?

_____

_____

How have I brought glory to God?

_____

_____

How have I added value to someone else's life?

_____

_____

What has been my experience with fasting?

_____

_____

_____

Challenge

This week is a double challenge.

Challenge 1: Choose a day this week to fast.

For most, fasting is the most difficult spiritual discipline. The act of denying our bodies something essential, like food, helps us develop the discipline to deny our sinful desires. Through fasting we show our complete devotion to God and His will.

Challenge 2: Choose a day this week to fast media.

You may need to pick a weekend, but choose a day to avoid your phone, social media, TV, etc. You can read, take a hike, hang out with a friend, or spend time in prayer. It's good to spend time detoxing our minds. We don't always realize the effect our electronic culture has on us until we take time away from it.

Use the "your notes" page this week to reflect on your experience with fasting. How did you feel? Was it as difficult as you thought it would be? How did you feel afterward? Do you feel closer to God as a result? How can you add fasting to your normal spiritual practice?

"Therefore God gave them over in the desires of their hearts to impurity, to dishonor their bodies among themselves. They exchanged the truth of God for a lie and worshiped and served the creation rather than the Creator, who is blessed forever! Amen."

Romans 1:24-25

Date: _____ _____

"The gospel is not a way to get people to heaven; it is a way to get people to God. It's a way of overcoming every obstacle to everlasting joy in God. If we don't want God above all things, we have not been converted by the gospel."
—John Piper

I am thankful for . . .

1. _____
2. _____
3. _____

God is calling me to be . . .

_____
_____
_____

I can serve God and others today by . . .

_____
_____
_____

My prayer for today is . . .

_____
_____
_____

☾

Where or how did I see God at work today?

_____
_____

What did I struggle with today that I want to overcome tomorrow?

_____
_____
_____

Your Notes

_____

_____

_____

_____

_____

_____

_____

_____

_____

_____

_____

_____

_____

_____

_____

_____

_____

_____

_____

_____

_____

_____

_____

_____

"Jesus replied, 'I am the way, and the truth, and the life. No one comes to the Father except through me. If you have known me, you will know my Father too. And from now on you do know him and have seen him.'"

John 14:6-7

Date:

"Suffering provides the gym equipment on which my faith can be exercised."
—*Joni Eareckson Tada*

I am thankful for . . .

1. _____
2. _____
3. _____

God is calling me to be . . .

_____
_____
_____

I can serve God and others today by . . .

_____
_____
_____

My prayer for today is . . .

_____
_____
_____

Where or how did I see God at work today?

_____
_____

What did I struggle with today that I want to overcome tomorrow?

_____
_____
_____

Your Notes

_____

_____

_____

_____

_____

_____

_____

_____

_____

_____

_____

_____

_____

_____

_____

_____

_____

_____

_____

_____

_____

_____

_____

"Therefore I am content with weaknesses, with insults, with troubles, with persecutions and difficulties for the sake of Christ, for whenever I am weak, then I am strong."

2 Corinthians 12:10

Date: _____ |———————————

> *"The things that we love tell us what we are."*
> *—Thomas Aquinas*

I am thankful for . . .

1. _____
2. _____
3. _____

God is calling me to be . . .

_____
_____
_____

I can serve God and others today by . . .

_____
_____
_____

My prayer for today is . . .

_____
_____
_____

🌙

Where or how did I see God at work today?

_____
_____

What did I struggle with today that I want to overcome tomorrow?

_____
_____
_____

Your Notes

_____

_____

_____

_____

_____

_____

_____

_____

_____

_____

_____

_____

_____

_____

_____

_____

_____

_____

_____

_____

_____

_____

_____

_____

"The good person out of the good treasury of his heart produces good, and the evil person out of his evil treasury produces evil, for his mouth speaks from what fills his heart."

Luke 6:45

"Riches and the things that are necessary in life are not evil in themselves. And all of us face cares and troubles in this life. The sin comes in the time and energy we spend in pursuing these things, at the expense of neglecting Christ."
—David Wilkerson

I am thankful for . . .

1. _____
2. _____
3. _____

God is calling me to be . . .

_____
_____
_____

I can serve God and others today by . . .

_____
_____
_____

My prayer for today is . . .

_____
_____
_____

Where or how did I see God at work today?

_____
_____

What did I struggle with today that I want to overcome tomorrow?

_____
_____
_____

Your Notes

_____
_____
_____
_____
_____
_____
_____
_____
_____
_____
_____
_____
_____
_____
_____
_____
_____
_____
_____
_____
_____
_____
_____
_____
_____

"No servant can serve two masters, for either he will hate the one and love the other, or he will be devoted to the one and despise the other. You cannot serve God and money."

Luke 16:13

"The joy of the Lord will arm us against the assaults of our spiritual enemies and put our mouths out of taste for those pleasures with which the tempter baits his hooks."
—Matthew Henry

I am thankful for . . .

1. _____
2. _____
3. _____

God is calling me to be . . .

_____
_____
_____

I can serve God and others today by . . .

_____
_____
_____

My prayer for today is . . .

_____
_____
_____

Where or how did I see God at work today?

_____
_____
_____

What did I struggle with today that I want to overcome tomorrow?

_____
_____
_____

Your Notes

_____

_____

_____

_____

_____

_____

_____

_____

_____

_____

_____

_____

_____

_____

_____

_____

_____

_____

_____

_____

_____

_____

_____

_____

_____

"You lead me in the path of life; I experience absolute joy in your presence; you always give me sheer delight."

Psalm 16:11

Date:

"Your greatest ministry will come out of your greatest obstacle.
God is able to recycle your pain for someone else's gain."
—Mark Batterson

I am thankful for . . .

1. _____
2. _____
3. _____

God is calling me to be . . .

_____
_____
_____

I can serve God and others today by . . .

_____
_____
_____

My prayer for today is . . .

_____
_____
_____

Where or how did I see God at work today?

_____
_____
_____

What did I struggle with today that I want to overcome tomorrow?

_____
_____
_____

Your Notes

_____

_____

_____

_____

_____

_____

_____

_____

_____

_____

_____

_____

_____

_____

_____

_____

_____

_____

_____

_____

_____

_____

_____

_____

_____

"But you know it was because of a physical illness that I first proclaimed the gospel to you, and though my physical condition put you to the test, you did not despise or reject me. Instead, you welcomed me as though I were an angel of God, as though I were Christ Jesus himself!"

Galatians 4:13-14

Weekly Growth Check-In

"It is the heart which perceives God and not the reason.
That is what faith is: God perceived by the heart, not by the reason."
—Blaise Pascal

In Christ, I am . . .

_____

_____

_____

What brought me joy last week?

_____

_____

_____

What might God be trying to speak to me through the events of the week?

_____

_____

_____

How have I brought glory to God?

_____

_____

_____

How have I added value to someone else's life?

_____

_____

_____

What talents, gifts, or abilities do I have that could be used to serve others?

_____

_____

_____

Challenge

Serve others this week using your unique gifts.

Your talents and abilities are the gifts you have which can be used to serve others. Don't feel pressured to serve in areas you're not gifted. Focus on your unique ability to add value to other people's lives. This will help you discover your role in the Body of Christ.

Go out of your way to serve as many people as you can this week. Constantly look for opportunities to serve others. Brainstorm to come up with some people and places where you know you could serve.

Use the "your notes" page this week to journal about what you think is your role in the Body of Christ. What has God created you for? Where can you best serve Him and His people?

"Now faith is being sure of what we hope for, being convinced of what we do not see."

Hebrews 11:1

"Forget being exotic and elite; it's all about becoming more like Christ."
—*John Ortberg*

I am thankful for . . .

1. _____
2. _____
3. _____

God is calling me to be . . .

_____
_____
_____

I can serve God and others today by . . .

_____
_____
_____

My prayer for today is . . .

_____
_____
_____

Where or how did I see God at work today?

_____
_____

What did I struggle with today that I want to overcome tomorrow?

_____
_____
_____

Your Notes

_____

_____

_____

_____

_____

_____

_____

_____

_____

_____

_____

_____

_____

_____

_____

_____

_____

_____

_____

_____

_____

_____

_____

_____

_____

"The one who says he resides in God ought himself to walk just as Jesus walked."

John 2:6

Date: _____ _____

"The gospel is not merely a 'belief system,' giving mental assent to 'sound doctrine'"so that one might 'go to heaven.' The gospel calls us to participate in the kingdom of heaven, to embody the will of God on earth, empowered by the Holy Spirit to do so."
—Lee Camp

I am thankful for . . .

1. _____
2. _____
3. _____

God is calling me to be . . .

_____
_____
_____

I can serve God and others today by . . .

_____
_____
_____

My prayer for today is . . .

_____
_____
_____

Where or how did I see God at work today?

_____
_____
_____

What did I struggle with today that I want to overcome tomorrow?

_____
_____
_____

Your Notes

_____

_____

_____

_____

_____

_____

_____

_____

_____

_____

_____

_____

_____

_____

_____

_____

_____

_____

_____

_____

_____

_____

_____

_____

"Therefore go and make disciples of all nations, baptizing them in the name of the Father and the Son and the Holy Spirit, teaching them to obey everything I have commanded you. And remember, I am with you always, to the end of the age."

Matthew 28:19-20

Date: _____ |—|

"In the early church, we see something of the community that understood its
identity as a people called to bear witness to the kingdom of God
in the midst of and for the sake of the world."
—Michael Goheen

I am thankful for . . .

1. _____
2. _____
3. _____

God is calling me to be . . .

_____
_____
_____

I can serve God and others today by . . .

_____
_____
_____

My prayer for today is . . .

_____
_____
_____

☾

Where or how did I see God at work today?

_____
_____
_____

What did I struggle with today that I want to overcome tomorrow?

_____
_____
_____

Your Notes

_____

_____

_____

_____

_____

_____

_____

_____

_____

_____

_____

_____

_____

_____

_____

_____

_____

_____

_____

_____

_____

_____

_____

_____

"They [the early church] were devoting themselves to the apostles' teaching and to fellowship, to the breaking of bread and to prayer. Reverential awe came over everyone, and many wonders and miraculous signs came about by the apostles."

Acts 2:42-43

Date: _____ |—————————————

"Cheap grace is the deadly enemy of our church.
We are fighting today for costly grace."
—Dietrich Bonhoeffer

I am thankful for . . .

1. _____
2. _____
3. _____

God is calling me to be . . .

_____
_____
_____

I can serve God and others today by . . .

_____
_____
_____

My prayer for today is . . .

_____
_____
_____

☾

Where or how did I see God at work today?

_____
_____

What did I struggle with today that I want to overcome tomorrow?

_____
_____
_____

Your Notes

_____
_____
_____
_____
_____
_____
_____
_____
_____
_____
_____
_____
_____
_____
_____
_____
_____
_____
_____
_____
_____
_____
_____
_____

"But God, being rich in mercy, because of his great love with which he loved us, even though we were dead in transgressions, made us alive together with Christ—by grace you are saved!"

Ephesians 2:4-5

"Being religious means asking passionately the question of the meaning of our existence and being willing to receive answers, even if the answers hurt."
—Paul Tillich

I am thankful for . . .

1. _____
2. _____
3. _____

God is calling me to be . . .

_____
_____
_____

I can serve God and others today by . . .

_____
_____
_____

My prayer for today is . . .

_____
_____
_____

☾

Where or how did I see God at work today?

_____
_____
_____

What did I struggle with today that I want to overcome tomorrow?

_____
_____
_____

Your Notes

_____
_____
_____
_____
_____
_____
_____
_____
_____
_____
_____
_____
_____
_____
_____
_____
_____
_____
_____
_____
_____
_____
_____
_____
_____

"And we know that all things work together for good for those who love God,
who are called according to his purpose."

Romans 8:28

Date: _____

"Our hope in life beyond death is a hope made possible, not by some general sentimental belief in life after death, but by our participation in the life of Christ."
—Stanley Hauerwas

I am thankful for . . .

1. _____
2. _____
3. _____

God is calling me to be . . .

_____
_____
_____

I can serve God and others today by . . .

_____
_____
_____

My prayer for today is . . .

_____
_____
_____

Where or how did I see God at work today?

_____
_____
_____

What did I struggle with today that I want to overcome tomorrow?

_____
_____
_____

Your Notes

_____

_____

_____

_____

_____

_____

_____

_____

_____

_____

_____

_____

_____

_____

_____

_____

_____

_____

_____

_____

_____

_____

_____

_____

"Enter through the narrow gate, because the gate is wide and the way is spacious that leads to destruction, and there are many who enter through it. How narrow is the gate and difficult the way that leads to life, and there are few who find it!"

Matthew 7:13-14

Weekly Growth Check-In

"I expect to pass through life but once. If therefore, there be any kindness that I can show, or any good thing I can do to any fellow being, let me do it now, and not defer or neglect it, as I shall not pass this way again."
—Stephen Grellet

In Christ, I am . . .

_____

_____

_____

What brought me joy last week?

_____

_____

What might God be trying to speak to me through the events of the week?

_____

_____

How have I brought glory to God?

_____

_____

How have I added value to someone else's life?

_____

_____

What in life brings me the most fulfillment? Why?

_____

_____

Challenge

Write a personal mission statement for your life.

Answering these questions can help you discover your life's purpose.

- What are you good at?
- What do you love doing?
- If you woke up tomorrow morning with no limitations, what would you do with the rest of your life?
- What once-in-a-lifetime opportunity would you most like to come along?
- Do you feel God has or is currently calling you to a specific vocation?
- Is there something standing in the way of you fulfilling what God has called you to do?
- What do you think is your life's purpose?

Look for obstacles that could be standing in your way of fulfilling your life's purpose. You may need to take action in order to eliminate obstacles keeping you from fulfilling your purpose. Or, maybe there isn't anything standing in your way and you just need to take action and start living the life you know God has called you to.

Use the "your notes" page this week to answer the questions above. Finish the week by writing out your own personal mission statement: "God has placed me on this earth to . . ."

"You do not know about tomorrow. What is your life like? For you are a puff of smoke that appears for a short time and then vanishes."

James 4:14

Date:

"Start by doing what's necessary; then do what's possible;
and suddenly you are doing the impossible."
—Francis of Assisi

I am thankful for . . .

1. _____

2. _____

3. _____

God is calling me to be . . .

_____

_____

_____

I can serve God and others today by . . .

_____

_____

_____

My prayer for today is . . .

_____

_____

_____

🌙

Where or how did I see God at work today?

_____

_____

What did I struggle with today that I want to overcome tomorrow?

_____

_____

_____

Your Notes

_____
_____
_____
_____
_____
_____
_____
_____
_____
_____
_____
_____
_____
_____
_____
_____
_____
_____
_____
_____
_____
_____
_____
_____
_____
_____

"He replied, 'What is impossible for mere humans is possible for God.'"

Luke 18:27

Date: _____ |—————————————

"You make a living by what you get; you make a life by what you give."
—Winston Churchill

✺

I am thankful for . . .

1. _____
2. _____
3. _____

God is calling me to be . . .

_____

_____

_____

I can serve God and others today by . . .

_____

_____

_____

My prayer for today is . . .

_____

_____

_____

☾

Where or how did I see God at work today?

_____

_____

_____

What did I struggle with today that I want to overcome tomorrow?

_____

_____

_____

Your Notes

_____
_____
_____
_____
_____
_____
_____
_____
_____
_____
_____
_____
_____
_____
_____
_____
_____
_____
_____
_____
_____
_____
_____
_____

"By all these things, I have shown you that by working in this way we must help the weak, and remember the words of the Lord Jesus that he himself said, 'It is more blessed to give than to receive.'"

Acts 20:35

Date: _____ |——————————

"Our confidence in Christ does not make us lazy, negligent, or careless, but on the contrary it awakens us, urges us on, and makes us active in living righteous lives and doing good. There is no self-confidence to compare with this."
—Huldrych Zwingli

I am thankful for . . .

1. _____
2. _____
3. _____

God is calling me to be . . .

_____
_____
_____

I can serve God and others today by . . .

_____
_____
_____

My prayer for today is . . .

_____
_____
_____

☾

Where or how did I see God at work today?

_____
_____
_____

What did I struggle with today that I want to overcome tomorrow?

_____
_____
_____

Your Notes

_____

_____

_____

_____

_____

_____

_____

_____

_____

_____

_____

_____

_____

_____

_____

_____

_____

_____

_____

_____

_____

_____

_____

"But I say, live by the Spirit and you will not carry out the desires of the flesh."

Galatians 5:16

Date: _____

"The Church exists by mission, just as a fire exists by burning.
Where there is no mission there is no Church;
and where there is neither Church nor mission, there is no faith."
—*Emil Brunner*

I am thankful for . . .

1. _____
2. _____
3. _____

God is calling me to be . . .

_____
_____
_____

I can serve God and others today by . . .

_____
_____
_____

My prayer for today is . . .

_____
_____
_____

🌙

Where or how did I see God at work today?

_____
_____
_____

What did I struggle with today that I want to overcome tomorrow?

_____
_____
_____

Your Notes

_____

_____

_____

_____

_____

_____

_____

_____

_____

_____

_____

_____

_____

_____

_____

_____

_____

_____

_____

_____

_____

_____

_____

_____

_____

_____

_____

"How are they to call on one they have not believed in? And how are they
to believe in one they have not heard of? And how are they to hear without
someone preaching to them? And how are they to preach unless they are sent? As
it is written, "How timely is the arrival of those who proclaim the good news."

Romans 10:14-15

Date:

"May the Living God, who is the portion and rest of the saints, make these our carnal minds so spiritual, and our earthly hearts so heavenly, that loving Him, and delighting in Him, may be the work or our lives."
—Richard Baxter

I am thankful for . . .

1. _____
2. _____
3. _____

God is calling me to be . . .

_____
_____
_____

I can serve God and others today by . . .

_____
_____
_____

My prayer for today is . . .

_____
_____
_____

Where or how did I see God at work today?

_____
_____
_____

What did I struggle with today that I want to overcome tomorrow?

_____
_____
_____

Your Notes

_____
_____
_____
_____
_____
_____
_____
_____
_____
_____
_____
_____
_____
_____
_____
_____
_____
_____
_____
_____
_____
_____
_____
_____

"Then you will take delight in the Lord, and he will answer your prayers."

Psalm 37:4

Date: _____ _____

"When it comes to Christianity we're all following the same Jesus (or at least should be) but that doesn't mean all of our paths will be the same. Don't compare your road to someone else's."
—Judah Smith

I am thankful for . . .

1. _____

2. _____

3. _____

God is calling me to be . . .

_____

_____

_____

I can serve God and others today by . . .

_____

_____

_____

My prayer for today is . . .

_____

_____

_____

Where or how did I see God at work today?

_____

_____

What did I struggle with today that I want to overcome tomorrow?

_____

_____

_____

Your Notes

_____

_____

_____

_____

_____

_____

_____

_____

_____

_____

_____

_____

_____

_____

_____

_____

_____

_____

_____

_____

_____

_____

_____

_____

"He gave me reason to sing a new song, praising our God. May many see what God has done, so that they might swear allegiance to him and trust in the Lord!"

Psalm 40:3

Weekly Growth Check-In

*"What lies behind us and what lies before us are
tiny matters compared to what lies within us."*
—Henry S. Haskins

In Christ, I am . . .

_____

_____

_____

What brought me joy last week?

_____

_____

What might God be trying to speak to me through the events of the week?

_____

_____

How have I brought glory to God?

_____

_____

How have I added value to someone else's life?

_____

_____

*Who is someone I look up to as a spiritual leader?
What is it that makes them a hero to me?*

_____

_____

Challenge

Look for a potential mentor this week.

When it comes to growth, there is no substitute for a good mentor. This could be a person who can help you in your spiritual growth like a pastor or leader in your church. Or, they could be a professional mentor who could help guide you on the vocational path God has called you to.

Reach out to a potential mentor this week by asking them for two or three books they would most recommend reading for success in the area that interests you.

This is a great way to initiate the mentor/mentee relationship without being pushy. Develop a relationship with your potential mentor before asking them to formally mentor you.

Use the "your notes" page this week to reflect on who you would most like to learn from as a mentor? Why do you want to learn from them? What do they have to offer that others don't? What about them do you most admire? Why?

"But the Lord said to him, 'Now you Pharisees clean the outside of the cup and the plate, but inside you are full of greed and wickedness. You fools! Didn't the one who made the outside make the inside as well? But give from your heart to those in need, and then everything will be clean for you.'"

Luke 11:39-41

Date: _____ ⊢_____

*"We weren't meant to walk alone. We are meant to walk with others in
community, sharing one another's burdens."*
—Anonymous

I am thankful for . . .

1. _____
2. _____
3. _____

God is calling me to be . . .

_____
_____
_____

I can serve God and others today by . . .

_____
_____
_____

My prayer for today is . . .

_____
_____
_____

☾

Where or how did I see God at work today?

_____
_____

What did I struggle with today that I want to overcome tomorrow?

_____
_____
_____

Your Notes

_____
_____
_____
_____
_____
_____
_____
_____
_____
_____
_____
_____
_____
_____
_____
_____
_____
_____
_____
_____
_____
_____
_____
_____

"Instead of being motivated by selfish ambition or vanity, each of you should, in humility, be moved to treat one another as more important than yourself."

Philippian 2:3

Date: _____ _____

"If we grow wiser and more learned in our intercourse with wise and learned persons, how much more will we gain in our inner life by communing with God in prayer."
—Huldrych Zwingli

I am thankful for . . .

1. _____
2. _____
3. _____

God is calling me to be . . .

_____
_____
_____

I can serve God and others today by . . .

_____
_____
_____

My prayer for today is . . .

_____
_____
_____

Where or how did I see God at work today?

_____
_____
_____

What did I struggle with today that I want to overcome tomorrow?

_____
_____
_____

Your Notes

_____
_____
_____
_____
_____
_____
_____
_____
_____
_____
_____
_____
_____
_____
_____
_____
_____
_____
_____
_____
_____
_____
_____
_____
_____

"Do not be wise in your own estimation; fear the Lord and turn away from evil."

Proverbs 3:7

*"Everything that irritates us about others
can lead us to an understanding of ourselves."*
—Carl Jung

I am thankful for . . .

1. _____
2. _____
3. _____

God is calling me to be . . .

_____
_____
_____

I can serve God and others today by . . .

_____
_____
_____

My prayer for today is . . .

_____
_____
_____

☾

Where or how did I see God at work today?

_____
_____

What did I struggle with today that I want to overcome tomorrow?

_____
_____
_____

Your Notes

_____

_____

_____

_____

_____

_____

_____

_____

_____

_____

_____

_____

_____

_____

_____

_____

_____

_____

_____

_____

_____

_____

_____

"Why do you see the speck in your brother's eye, but fail to see the beam of wood in your own? Or how can you say to your brother, 'Let me remove the speck from your eye,' while there is a beam in your own? You hypocrite! First remove the beam from your own eye, and then you can see clearly to remove the speck from your brother's eye."

Matthew 7:3-5

"I don't think the greatest threat to Christianity is radical terrorism.
I think it's nominal Christians."
—Nabeel Qureshi

I am thankful for . . .

1. _____
2. _____
3. _____

God is calling me to be . . .

_____
_____
_____

I can serve God and others today by . . .

_____
_____
_____

My prayer for today is . . .

_____
_____
_____

Where or how did I see God at work today?

_____
_____

What did I struggle with today that I want to overcome tomorrow?

_____
_____
_____

Your Notes

_____
_____
_____
_____
_____
_____
_____
_____
_____
_____
_____
_____
_____
_____
_____
_____
_____
_____
_____
_____
_____
_____
_____
_____

"So because you are lukewarm, and neither hot nor cold, I am going to vomit you out of my mouth!"

Revelation 3:16

Date: _____

"To gather with God's people in united adoration of the Father is as necessary to the Christian life as prayer."
—*Martin Luther*

I am thankful for . . .

1. _____
2. _____
3. _____

God is calling me to be . . .

_____
_____
_____

I can serve God and others today by . . .

_____
_____
_____

My prayer for today is . . .

_____
_____
_____

Where or how did I see God at work today?

_____
_____
_____

What did I struggle with today that I want to overcome tomorrow?

_____
_____
_____

Your Notes

_____

_____

_____

_____

_____

_____

_____

_____

_____

_____

_____

_____

_____

_____

_____

_____

_____

_____

_____

_____

_____

_____

_____

_____

"And let us take thought of how to spur one another on to love and good works, not abandoning our own meetings, as some are in the habit of doing, but encouraging each other, and even more so because you see the day drawing near."

Hebrews 10:24-25

Date: _____ ⊢_____

"Grace must find expression in life, otherwise it is not grace."
—Karl Barth

☀

I am thankful for . . .

1. _____
2. _____
3. _____

God is calling me to be . . .

_____
_____
_____

I can serve God and others today by . . .

_____
_____
_____

My prayer for today is . . .

_____
_____
_____

☾

Where or how did I see God at work today?

_____
_____

What did I struggle with today that I want to overcome tomorrow?

_____
_____
_____

Your Notes

_____

_____

_____

_____

_____

_____

_____

_____

_____

_____

_____

_____

_____

_____

_____

_____

_____

_____

_____

_____

_____

_____

_____

_____

_____

"I have been crucified with Christ, and it is no longer I who live, but Christ lives in me. So the life I now live in the body, I live because of the faithfulness of the Son of God, who loved me and gave himself for me."

Galatians 2:20

Weekly Growth Check-In

"You must never sacrifice your relationship with God
for the sake of a relationship with another person."
—Charles Stanley

In Christ, I am . . .

_____

_____

_____

What brought me joy last week?

_____

_____

What might God be trying to speak to me through the events of the week?

_____

_____

How have I brought glory to God?

_____

_____

How have I added value to someone else's life?

_____

_____

What qualities am I working to develop in my life?

_____

_____

Challenge

Become the leader God has called you to be.

We can all be leaders in our own lives. Leadership involves the courage to step out and live your life on display so others can follow. Leadership is about serving others, not self-aggrandizement.

Instead of focusing on yourself, look for an opportunity to lead someone this week by encouraging them or affirming their role in the Body of Christ. Whether they serve in front of people or behind the scenes, you can serve them by affirming who they are and what they do.

Use the "your notes" page this week to journal about what you think your role as a leader means for those you serve. You may not lead thousands, but you can influence those around you. How does your behavior affect them? How does seeing yourself as a leader change your perspective? Are you comfortable being a leader? Why or why not?

"If anyone comes to me and does not hate his own father and mother, and wife and children, and brothers and sisters, and even his own life, he cannot be my disciple."

Luke 14:26

Date: _____

"If your Gospel isn't touching others, it hasn't touched you!"
—Curry R. Blake

✸

I am thankful for . . .

1. _____
2. _____
3. _____

God is calling me to be . . .

_____
_____
_____

I can serve God and others today by . . .

_____
_____
_____

My prayer for today is . . .

_____
_____
_____

☾

Where or how did I see God at work today?

_____
_____
_____

What did I struggle with today that I want to overcome tomorrow?

_____
_____
_____

Your Notes

_____
_____
_____
_____
_____
_____
_____
_____
_____
_____
_____
_____
_____
_____
_____
_____
_____
_____
_____
_____
_____
_____
_____
_____
_____
_____

"But be sure you live out the message and do not merely listen to it and so deceive yourselves."

James 1:22

Date: _____ _____

"Man should not consider his material possession his own, but as common to all, so as to share them without hesitation when others are in need."
—*Thomas Aquinas*

I am thankful for . . .

1. _____
2. _____
3. _____

God is calling me to be . . .

_____
_____
_____

I can serve God and others today by . . .

_____
_____
_____

My prayer for today is . . .

_____
_____
_____

☾

Where or how did I see God at work today?

_____
_____
_____

What did I struggle with today that I want to overcome tomorrow?

_____
_____
_____

Your Notes

"For there was no one needy among them, because those who were owners of land or houses were selling them and bringing the proceeds from the sales and placing them at the apostles' feet. The proceeds were distributed to each, as anyone had need."

Acts 4:34-35

*"I see with greater and greater clearness that consistent
Christianity is the easiest Christianity to defend."*
—John Gresham Machen

I am thankful for . . .

1. _____
2. _____
3. _____

God is calling me to be . . .

_____
_____
_____

I can serve God and others today by . . .

_____
_____
_____

My prayer for today is . . .

_____
_____
_____

☾

Where or how did I see God at work today?

_____
_____

What did I struggle with today that I want to overcome tomorrow?

_____
_____
_____

Your Notes

_____

_____

_____

_____

_____

_____

_____

_____

_____

_____

_____

_____

_____

_____

_____

_____

_____

_____

_____

_____

_____

_____

_____

"People do not light a lamp and put it under a basket but on a lampstand, and it gives light to all in the house. In the same way, let your light shine before people, so that they can see your good deeds and give honor to your Father in heaven."

Matthew 5:15-16

Date: _____ _____

"A truth said with bad intentions or not delivered
in love can sour people to the truth."
—Josh Havens

I am thankful for . . .

1. _____
2. _____
3. _____

God is calling me to be . . .

_____
_____
_____

I can serve God and others today by . . .

_____
_____
_____

My prayer for today is . . .

_____
_____
_____

☾

Where or how did I see God at work today?

_____
_____
_____

What did I struggle with today that I want to overcome tomorrow?

_____
_____
_____

Your Notes

_____

_____

_____

_____

_____

_____

_____

_____

_____

_____

_____

_____

_____

_____

_____

_____

_____

_____

_____

_____

_____

_____

_____

_____

_____

"Everything you do should be done in love."

1 Corinthians 16:14

Date:

"If God is the Creator of the entire universe, then it must follow that He is the Lord of the whole universe. No part of the world is outside of His lordship. That means that no part of my life must be outside of His lordship."
—*R.C. Sproul*

I am thankful for . . .

1. _____
2. _____
3. _____

God is calling me to be . . .

_____
_____
_____

I can serve God and others today by . . .

_____
_____
_____

My prayer for today is . . .

_____
_____
_____

Where or how did I see God at work today?

_____
_____
_____

What did I struggle with today that I want to overcome tomorrow?

_____
_____
_____

Your Notes

_____
_____
_____
_____
_____
_____
_____
_____
_____
_____
_____
_____
_____
_____
_____
_____
_____
_____
_____
_____
_____
_____
_____
_____
_____
_____

"Listen, Israel: The Lord is our God, the Lord is one! You must love the Lord your God with your whole mind, your whole being, and all your strength."

Deuteronomy 6:4-5

Date: _____ _____

"Our opportunities to do good are our talents."
—*Cotton Mather*

I am thankful for . . .

1. _____
2. _____
3. _____

God is calling me to be . . .

_____
_____
_____

I can serve God and others today by . . .

_____
_____
_____

My prayer for today is . . .

_____
_____
_____

Where or how did I see God at work today?

_____
_____

What did I struggle with today that I want to overcome tomorrow?

_____
_____
_____

Your Notes

_____

_____

_____

_____

_____

_____

_____

_____

_____

_____

_____

_____

_____

_____

_____

_____

_____

_____

_____

_____

_____

_____

_____

_____

"Just as each one has received a gift, use it to serve one another as good stewards of the varied grace of God."

1 Peter 4:10

Daily Growth for the Future

How would you best describe your mission statement in life?

_____

_____

_____

_____

What do you feel is your role in the Body of Christ? How can you best serve others?

_____

_____

_____

_____

How do you currently feel about your relationship with Christ?

_____

_____

_____

_____

What affect has this journal had your walk with Christ?

_____

_____

_____

_____

What can you do to ensure continued growth in your walk with Christ?

_____

_____

_____

_____

Congratulations on completing the Daily Growth Journal!

Words can't express how proud I am that you have completed this journal. I'm sure you have grown in your walk with Christ because of your commitment and discipline to stick with this amazing discipline.

You may be asking yourself, "Now what?" I hope you'll use the principles in the DGJ as you continue your journey with Christ.

Perhaps you have established the discipline of journaling so well that you can begin a traditional journal. Even though the DGJ focused on the most important areas of the Christian life, they were only a small selection of the areas to explore if you want to grow in your walk with Christ. A traditional journal will let you branch out and explore other avenues of the Christian life. Of course, you can always start a new DGJ and customize it to further meet your needs.

Since you've already established the discipline of journaling, don't break that habit by taking a "break" from journaling. That will only make it harder for you to get back into the discipline.

I hope you have developed a love and a passion for this amazing spiritual discipline. I pray that God will continue to lead and guide you in His will so you make the greatest impact for the kingdom of God that you can. As my final words to you, I would like to remind you that we don't grow spiritually only for ourselves. We grow in the Lord so that we can better serve others. Now get out there and serve others by sharing what God has done in your life!

"Lord, may you ignite a passion in their heart for taking the gospel to their neighbor. May your Holy Spirit empower them to serve even their enemies. Continue to mold them into the perfect image of Jesus, so that when people look at them, they see You. I pray they will be disciples who make other disciples. Lead and guide them down the path You have ordained for them. May You use them to affect change for the kingdom of God, as they are continually transformed by the power of Your Holy Spirit. Amen!"

References

Augustine. *The City of God*, Volume 2. Coterie Classics, 2016, 319.

Bonhoeffer, Dietrich. *The Cost of Discipleship*. New York, NY: Touchstone, 1959, 43.

Baxter, Richard. *The Saint's Everlasting Rest*. Grand Rapids, MI: Baker, 1978, 17.

Chambers, Oswald. *Utmost: Classic Readings and Prayers from Oswald Chambers*. Grand Rapids, MI: Discovery House Publishers, 2012.

Camp, Lee. *Mere Discipleship: Radical Christianity in a Rebellious World*. Grand Rapids, MI: Brazos Press, 2008, 133.

Chan, Francis. *Crazy Love: Overwhelmed by a Relentless God*. Colorado Springs, CO: David C. Cook, 2008.

Foster, Richard. *Celebration of Discipline: The Path to Spiritual Growth*. Revised Edition. New York, NY: HarperCollins, 1988.

Goheen, Michael. *A Light to the Nations: The Missional Church and the Biblical Story*. Grand Rapids, MI: Baker Academic, 2011, 8.

Goldsworthy, Graeme. *According to Plan: The Unfolding Revelation of God in the Bible*. Downers Grove, IL: IVP Academic, 2002, 91.

Graham, Billy. *Peace with God: The Secret of Happiness*. Nashville, TN: Thomas Nelson, 2011.

Guinness, Os. *In Two Minds: The Dilemma of Doubt & How to Resolve It*. Downers Grove, IL: InterVarsity Press, 1976, 168.

Mather, Cotton. *Essays to Do Good*. Glasgow: Chalmers and Collins, 1825, 69.

Henry, Matthew. *An Exposition of the Old and New Testament*. Volume 2. London: Joseph Robinson, 1839, 1096.

Jung, Carl. *Memories, Dreams, Reflections*. New York: NY: Random House, 1989.

Keller, Timothy. *The Reason for God: Belief in an Age of Skepticism*. New York, NY: Viking Books, 2008.

McKnight, Scot. *One Life: Jesus Calls, We Follow*. Grand Rapids, MI: Zondervan, 2010, 100.

Nouwen, Henri. *Seeds of Hope*. Image Books, 1997.

Piper, John. *God Is the Gospel: Meditations on God's Love as the Gift of Himself*. Wheaton, IL: Crossway Books, 2005.

Platt, David. *Radical: Taking Back Your Faith from the American Dream.* Colorado Springs, CO: Multnomah Books, 2010, 94.

Schaff, Philip. *History of the Christian Church*, Volume 1. Arkose Press, 2015, 574.

Stanley, Charles. *Charles Stanley's Handbook for Christian Living: Biblical Answers to Life's Tough Questions.* Nashville, TN: Thomas Nelson, 2008, 409.

Tada, Joni Eareckson. *Making Sense of Suffering.* Peabody, MA: Aspire Press, 2013.

Tillich, Paul. *The Essential Tillich.* Chicago, IL: The University of Chicago Press, 1987, 1.

Wright, Christopher J.H. *The Mission of God: Unlocking the Bible's Grand Narrative.* Downers Grove, IL: InterVarsity Press, 2006, 23.

_____. *Salvation Belongs to Our God: Celebrating the Bible's Central Story.* Downers Grove, IL: InterVarsity Press, 2008, 181.

Yancey, Philip. *Where is God When It Hurts: A Comforting, Healing Guide for Coping with Hard Times.* Grand Rapids, MI: Zondervan, 1990, 232.

Yoder, John H. *The Politics of Jesus.* Grand Rapids, MI: Eerdmans, 1994, 51.

If this journal has been helpful to you, please consider passing on the gift of spiritual growth by telling someone about your experience using the journal. I would also love to hear your story.

You can email me at: **dailygrowthdiscipleship@gmail.com**.

Made in the USA
Columbia, SC
28 October 2017